The Messy in the Middle

Stephanie L. McWhorter

authorHOUSE®

AuthorHouse™
1663 Liberty Drive
Bloomington, IN 47403
www.authorhouse.com
Phone: 833-262-8899

Published by AuthorHouse 08/23/2022

ISBN: 978-1-6655-6597-4 (sc)
ISBN: 978-1-6655-6595-0 (hc)
ISBN: 978-1-6655-6596-7 (e)

Library of Congress Control Number: 2022913586

Print information available on the last page.

DEDICATION

To my sweet Aleah Joy:

I will never forget holding you in my arms while my therapist prayed that you and I would share a close, unbreakable bond through such a difficult storm in our lives.

And we do.

But I am never blind to the fact that the storm for you, even as you are now a nine-year-old child, is different than the storm for me.

This is a storm I never wanted you to have to face, because I know as you grow older, life will bring you many more storms.

My prayer, however, is that you will cling to your faith now and in the future when life hands you messy situations and places.

You are my forever sunshine and I love you so much,

Love, Mommy!

To my sweet Nyla:

You are never far from my heart and you are never absent from my story. I carry you with me always. I pray that you are in heaven proud of how I tell your story, each time that I tell it. Thank you for being the angel that I know prays when your mommy and little sister are hurting. You still make me proud.

You are my forever angel and I love you so much,

Love, Mommy!

PREFACE

"God, what in the world are you doing?!"

I'm just going to be honest and say that's the most frequently asked question in my car lately, when I'm all by myself, and there's nobody but me and him.

My grandmother would be so ashamed of me.

I know she told me not to question him. I know she told me not to ask him why. But some of the things that he does. Some of the things he allows. They leave me all puzzled.

And I'm just stuck trying to figure out what he sees that I don't that could somehow make this chapter in my life okay.

Am I the only one?

Maybe. I don't know.

But sometimes, I have doubts.

And I thought I should start this book off by saying that upfront.

Sometimes, I don't get God.

And that's why being unfinished sucks.

I know. I know. This is a Christian book and it's not starting off so great.

The author is questioning God. Saying she doesn't get him. And now, she uses the word, "suck."

But don't you use it too, sometimes, when you're all alone and trying to figure out life?

Don't you use it when you are driving on the road, trying to make it to your next meeting, and all of a sudden, get a nail in your tire?

Or maybe then, you use worse words.

Can I be honest?

I think the world is starving for more real Christians.

Not irreverent Christians.

Not loose Christians.

But real Christians.

Those who will say, "Yes, I love God. He's good to me. I have a personal relationship with Him that transcends church and people."

But sometimes, life still hurts.

And because I have this relationship with God, I sometimes wonder if he sees just how bad I hurt.

Real Christians.

Real Christians who can sit down at a table and admit when they believed God and expected God to come through in one way, and he didn't, they became a little discouraged.

Real Christians.

Real Christians who can say, yes, my makeup is flawless. And my hair is laid. I look put together, but my heart has so many holes in it, that's it's all I can do just to sit here and look you in the eye, today.

Real Christians.

Because when we have real Christians that are willing to admit that no matter how flawless things look on the outside, we are all broken on the inside, it helps us not feel alone.

So, friend, here I am. Real. Raw. And naked. In heart, of course.

I love God. I know that God loves me.

But sometimes, I am doing all I can just to hold it together.

My life right now is a little messy.

Take that back. Who am I kidding?

My life right now is completely messy.

But you know what, I believe there's purpose in the mess.

Just like a good ole peanut butter and jelly sandwich.

We've all got to admit, that without that sticky, messy, gooey combination of peanut butter and jelly in the middle, those two pieces of bread on the outside wouldn't taste nearly as good.

And that's what I believe the messiness in our lives does.

It gives us a story.

It gives us the goodness in our lives.

And I know right now, we're in the middle of something hard.

And so, finding goodness doesn't seem as easy now.

But friend, good can come out of our messy middle.

And when we give it to God, good will come out of our messy middle.

But that's not where we're going to start our journey.

We're not going to get spiritual before we get real.

Because sometimes we say spiritual things with our mouths that our hearts don't yet believe.

And yes, I believe that it's good to speak a thing before you see a thing.

But I also believe that God cares about what's really in our hearts when we are broken, hurting, and disappointed.

He cares that we feel a mess when our life is a mess.

So, grab a few tissues.

Grab a journal.

And get ready to pour out your heart to God.

Because I believe he wants to heal your heart right there in your messy middle.

CHAPTER 1

A Messy Realization

I knew it was over.

I had been fighting for so long to save it. Praying for God to work a miracle. Putting to use every piece of advice I received in a counseling session.

And for a while, it all seemed great.

"Wow!" "God is really doing this," I thought. "What a miracle worker."

Except, on that day, it wasn't a miracle anymore.

It was a disaster. My marriage of twelve years, over.

And I was heartbroken.

Heartbroken that it was over.

Heartbroken because I felt God had let me down.

Heartbroken because I couldn't protect my child from the realities of divorce that I experienced when I was a child.

Heartbroken that the guy that I fought for and believed in could so easily choose to walk away from me, again.

Yep, I said it. Again.

That was the hardest part.

Believing the best about someone who so easily disregarded my love. Not once. But multiple times.

Now, if that isn't heartbreak.

But this isn't about him.

It's about me. And my heart.

All the things that was wrong with it then.

All the things still going on in it, now.

And why being stuck in the middle of this season is so darn hard.

Because nothing is harder than over, ya'll. Nothing.

A marriage you put your all into.

Over.

A career you worked so hard to build.

Over.

A project you so passionately pursued.

Over.

Over can bring pain.

Even if over is a good thing.

Being over something as damaging as a drug habit would in fact be a good thing.

Except, withdrawal is painful. And long.

And yes, when it's over, there is clarity.

But in the middle, it sucks.

Hmmm… I'm beginning to think that should've been the title of this book.

Okay, so maybe, not. But…how many of you would've still picked up this book with a title like that.

I know for sure, I would've.

Because, the middle. The uncertain spaces in time. The time where you're not there, as in where you used to be, but you're also not there either, as in where you want to be. Those places just don't make sense.

And so, we need God, right in the middle.

When things end.

Things that we wanted to stay. And things that needed to go.

We need him right in the middle.

Where pain exists.

When uncertainty persist.

Where footing is unsure.

Where voices of doubt ring louder than voices of truth.

In the middle.

When we are unsure of what tomorrow looks like.

And we are unsure of what today will bring, we need Jesus. More of Him. And a lot less of us.

A lot less of what we think and feel. And a lot more of who he says we are and what he calls us to believe.

We need him to fill the spaces in our heart that say that what we're believing for will never happen. We need for him to speak his assurance into the places that tell us we will never become who he says we are to be.

In the middle. It's where we need him most.

So, as we're reading together, we're also searching together. For God. Right in the middle.

CHAPTER 2

Messy Acceptance

It was the week before my daughter started Kindergarten and I was attending her orientation.

Kindergarten.

It should've been an exciting year for so many reasons.

It was the first time I would experience getting to see a child go to Kindergarten. My oldest daughter graduated from earth and went to heaven when she was just three.

So, I should've been excited to see my second child begin kindergarten.

But instead, I was disillusioned.

Just four weeks before this date, my family had been suddenly ripped to shreds. And there I was, sitting at orientation, happy just to take a break from running amuck, signing leases, getting her into a new school just before the semester began, and making sure that I didn't accidentally put the wrong address on her forms.

I remember looking around the room at all of the families of kindergarteners and thinking "It's not supposed to be this way."

I've bet you've said that a time or two before, too.

Maybe you've looked at your bank account in the red after having had years of successful business and thought, "It's not supposed to be this way."

Maybe you've looked into an empty crib in a room you prepared for your baby who was stillborn and thought, "It's not supposed to be this way."

Maybe, you've looked around your house and into the face of the children you love and adored and felt the aching nudge of unfulfillment and dissatisfaction in your heart and thought, "It's not supposed to be this way."

Maybe, you've sat in a movie theatre and cried your eyes out after an extended shopping spree, because your spouse works and makes good money, but you feel alone, and, "It's not supposed to be this way."

So many times, we judge the emptiness in others, because it's not what we would call empty. But the truth is, we all have empty spaces.

And while the emptiness in them may not be the emptiness in you, somewhere in their life, they too, think, "It's not supposed to be this way."

And many times, this is the thinking that stops us.

Because we have this idea. This idea that the euphoric life we dream of when we are young school kids will play out exactly as we imagined.

And even when we grow up and realize that life isn't quite that way, when our resilience to pursue our dreams and our heart's desires continuously meets life's resistance, we can sometimes give in to permanent resignation, all the while, thinking that the way things are isn't exactly how they're supposed to be.

But afraid to try again.

Because, darn it. That wall. That resistance. That failure. That disappointment. That middle.

It hurts.

And you know what, I get it.

I'm a girl who's had more failures than I care to count with you.

More setbacks than I'd care to replay.

More resistance than I'd care to reimagine.

But, you know what. I don't know about you, but I still have something in me that tells me that what it is today, is not the way it's supposed to be forever.

I've still got something in me that tells me that while disappointment is a part of my life, disappointment is not all there is to my life.

For a while, I thought that I gained this perspective from people. From others in my life who God placed around me to remind me that I still had purpose and needed to keep going. And I have to tell you, they were definitely a part of it.

But in reality, the part of me that was screaming in discontentment was the part of me that already knew it.

The part of me that wanted so desperately to end life, but instead decided to keep living life anyway. Even though she was discouraged and greatly wounded, she was the person inside of me screaming, "This is not it."

She was the person screaming, "Don't give up, yet."

She was the person screaming, "It's *not* supposed to be this way."

But not just in the way that says, this shouldn't be my life.

She was also screaming, "It's not supposed to be this way," in a way that said, this ending is not God's ending.

There's more.

And that same voice is in you, too.

Screaming. This is not God's ending.

There's a voice in you that's a friend to your destiny and not your disappointment.

There's a voice in you that's a friend to your purpose and not your pain, and it's calling you beyond what is now into what it will be then.

It's calling you beyond what you see into what God sees.

It's calling you beyond your limited view, into God's vision.

And that's the journey we're going to take together, friend.

Through the messy into the beautiful.

CHAPTER 3

Messy Places

For the longest time, I have dreamed of giving birth.

It's an experience I've not had, yet.

But I've got a few friends who have given birth. And their stories are often, well…scary!

I've had friends with difficult pregnancies and difficult births. And I've had friends with easy pregnancies and easy births.

But I don't think I've ever heard anyone describe their experience to me as "beautiful."

Even those with easy pregnancies and easy births describe some discomfort.

Because holding a life, growing a life, and birthing a life is a process.

And sometimes, a messy process.

Because in that room, on that table, there's a lot going on. A lot of breathing. A lot of pain, for some. Possibly some four- letter words being said, for some. Hey, God knows how much it hurts.

And…there's a lot of pushing.

Pushing that engages muscles that we often use to push out some other stuff. Some messy, stinky, stuff.

And even if your baby is delivered by way of C-section, oh, it gets messy. I've seen the video of doctors cutting through multiple layers of skin and shifting organs. It gets messy.

Life doesn't usually hand us the beautiful without the messy.

And while that may be a daunting statement for many, it's also a beautiful promise.

A promise that if a mess currently exist in your life right now, that somewhere peeping through is some beauty.

And so, what I want you to know right now, is that even if you feel like saying four letter words good Christians don't say, or if your mental and emotional muscles are sore from pushing through the messes of life, even if it feels like your organs have been pulled out and put back inside, know this, there is beauty on the other side.

I know you can't see it now. Neither can I.

But do me this one favor and commit to take the journey of seeing it through.

Because some of life's best stories come from messy places.

CHAPTER 4

An uneasy mess

I went to see a movie today. It's a movie I had been wanting to see since the day that it opened, which was about four days ago, so it's not like I've been waiting forever. But I had great anticipation for this movie. Produced by someone I'd been following for years and starring an actor I had grown to love since she had been newly introduced to me a few years ago. I could not wait!

And to add to all of those pluses, it was a movie in my favorite category. A romantic comedy.

I should've known better.

This movie brought out all of the feels.

The anger, hurt, and the sting of rejection from my current ending marriage.

The emotional therapy I needed when a scene in the movie addressed the tendency for women to sometimes suppress their emotions in order to keep pushing ahead.

Sex. Lots of sex. Innuendos. And scenes.

And ya'll know, for a woman fresh out of a season where doing all of those things was free, I needed Jesus to hold my reigns.

Immediately.

Because I wasn't prepared.

The facial expressions.

The intensity.

The fine man with his glistening muscles that were speaking to me from the movie scene.

And if you wonder if I am having flash backs and getting a little too detailed for this book that is supposed to be a Christian book, let me tell you that I am not. I am being specifically detailed on purpose.

Because so frequently, we want our books and our sermons and our songs to politely glide over the topics that make us squirm when we hear them in relation to our Christianity and our relationship with Christ, when these things are so very real in our daily life.

And yet, we act like it doesn't exist in church. I think we do that, so we can make it okay behind closed doors.

"True deliverance speaks things out loud, into the air and into community where there is accountability."

But true deliverance speaks things out loud, into the air and into community where there is accountability.

I am a Christian woman. I love Jesus with all of my heart. But I am also a human woman with a flesh that screams when it bumps up against temptation.

And even when I am doing my best to try to avoid it, sometimes, it catches me off guard. And the only way to beat it is to be brave enough to call it out.

But that's only one temptation.

So many more lurk beneath the surface.

Like the temptation to believe that what we see in movies is what life should look like in reality.

This movie I was watching, it was the typical romance story.

A girl whose heart had been broken had driven herself into a state of funk and depression. Meanwhile, this guy who had been interested in her all along recognizes that now is the time to step to her with his game, so to speak.

And it's like almost instantly after heartbreak, Mr. Right steps in and makes it all okay.

And while of course, the woman in the movie doesn't think he's a great guy, everybody watching sees differently.

He is definitely the guy that she should be with.

He definitely loves her with the kind of intensity and passion that every unmarried woman wishing to be married dreams of.

The end.

Happily ever after. Don't screw this up, girl. Everyone can see he's perfect for you.

Except, in real life, rarely does this happen. Rarely does a heartbreak in one season give way to joy in a new season immediately.

There's some pain in between. And not the kind of pain where your girlfriends bring over your favorite sparkly drink and some popcorn, and your cry it all out in one night, and then snap back the next day, either.

The in between season is painful. There is process. There are tears. There are moments of loneliness even when your friends are right there beside you holding your hand as you cry. There is confusion. There is doubt. There are long periods where all you hear from God is complete silence.

And if we don't learn to expect these moments. And to lean into them just as fiercely as we would lean into the scene where the girl gets the guy that's just perfect for her, we miss an important piece of the puzzle. And an important part of the story.

Because it's not in the ending that God gets the most glory. No, friends. It's in the middle.

It's in the waiting. The part of your story where you thought he wasn't coming. The part of the story where you had to be on the other side to really appreciate what he was doing for you when you look back.

That's the part that makes his glory shine most.

And married ladies. Or single and satisfied, ladies. Don't get trapped in all of the talk about sex and romance that you miss how this applies to you, too.

Maybe, it's the six-bedroom, three-and-a-half bathroom house that you've been dreaming of all of your life. Perhaps this sounds like a luxury to so many. But for you and the season you're in right now, it's what you're believing God for.

I visited some friends a few months back at their big, beautiful home for the very first time.

It looked like a dream.

Their backyard was humongous and extended for yards and yards and their downstairs living space looked like a second single-story home with a built-in bar.

But what I admired most about their home is the story behind it.

They never wanted a big home for show.

Instead, they wanted a place where they could do ministry and outreach.

The home they were dreaming of was about more than just the things they wanted; it was about the God they served and the people they wanted to serve.

And I share that story to say that what seems like luxury to some of us, isn't luxury to all of us.

And that's okay.

That's another friend thing.

We need to stop judging the person next to us simply for having more than us. Perhaps they are called to have more.

No, not because they're better than us. But because they have a calling that's different from us. And that's incredibly great. Because it's how we all fit together as one body in Christ.

And to the woman who is believing for more to serve others more, delay is just as painful.

But the glory, my friend, it's not in the house. It's in the moment you get to finally sit around a table with the people in your life and tell the story of how God made you wait, for better.

Yes, for better.

The glory, dear friend who is believing for God just to get you through this class with a passing grade, is not the grade itself, it's the story you get to tell all your friends about how you thought you were going to fail the entire semester, but somehow with faith, prayer, grace, and a lot of hard work, God did the impossible.

The glory of the story, friends, is never at the end. And many times, we never get to see the glory of story that easy.

There's a fight for deliverance. There's a fight for breakthrough. There's a process for healing.

Don't rush past it.

"There's a fight for deliverance. There's a fight for breakthrough. There's a process for healing. Don't rush past it."

CHAPTER 5

Embrace the Season

I did NOT want to be a single mom.

And I write that sentence knowing that some will read and identify, and others will read it and possibly be offended.

Please understand, there is nothing wrong with being a single mom, and I know that many of you that maybe did not choose it, have also grown to love it.

But that's not where I was when this pretty package of single parenting landed on my doorstep. I didn't choose it. I didn't want it. And I resented it.

Don't get me wrong. Not for a second did I resent my child. I cried for her, begged for her, pleaded with God for her on many, many occasions. She wasn't going anywhere.

But the burden of dealing with my own heartbreak, and hers, too, was overwhelming, and undesirable.

The burden of having it all on me most of the time was unwelcomed.

But ready or not, wanted or not, here it was.

And can I tell you something? I struggled. For a long while.

My child, who had always been clingy, overactive, and a little extra needy at times, now also came with the heartache and confusion of a broken family. And all she knew to do was show her confusion through her behavior.

And I, myself, was unhealed. And single. And overwhelmed. And sad. And angry.

Because the burden of this season was unfair. And unjust.

And so, I decided to ignore it all. Not to ignore my child, altogether. But I refused to embrace that I was in a new season of life that required more of me as a parent.

Because I didn't want it. And so, I wasn't going to accept it.

But the thing was that it wasn't going away.

Ignore as I might, the truth of the matter still remained. I was a one parent household with a child who needed me.

And I had to realize that. I had to accept that. I had to live in that.

But it didn't happen easily.

Before I could change my mind to parent, I had to first change my mind to stop resisting what God was doing in my life.

Because, I was so very angry at him.

And my anger was keeping me from the full surrender that provided the grace I needed to be able to embrace this new season fully.

And so, I had to deal with my God issues. And my trust issues. And my pride issues. And I had to fully surrender.

I had to not say that I trusted God with my mouth, while in my heart, I was relentlessly fighting him.

Have you ever been there? Maybe not as a single mom. But somewhere, in a season that God has called you to, that is completely against your will?

Listen, the answer starts with surrender. Not in words. Not even in actions. But in heart.

Because true surrender in your heart will guide your actions.

Heart surrender says," God, I give up my right to have this my way and I will trust you to lead the way."

And I know, it only sounds easy when it's put into a sentence.

The reality of it all is so much harder.

It's much harder when you are waiting for your career to take off, and it seems like God makes you the mentor of sorts to others, but you feel like he is pushing the halt button on your dreams.

When that's the case, surrender sucks.

Because it feels like God is just using you.

Hmmm… using you. You know, like so many of the songs we sing, say. "Use me, Lord. Not my will, but yours."

But a halt on what we want, or even a pause on what we want can seem like a crushing.

And a crushing seems like a breaking.

"True surrender in your heart will guide your actions."

And a breaking, sometimes in the moment, causes us to feel like we've been abandoned, cast aside, and forgotten.

Sometimes, the call from God to go deeper and come closer feels a lot like disappointment.

And we have to come to terms with that.

Because a changed heart starts with an honest heart.

And when we are honest about what's in our heart, God can heal it.

And he can help us to lean into the new thing, the now thing. The thing that he is working in the now.

And when we lean into it, we can find joy in the things that would've brought us heartache.

Because we aren't sulking over what we didn't get. And what we don't want.

But we are embracing where we are.

For me, this means walking in the truth that I am single mom. But not just a single mom. A chosen mom. A mom that God has seen so much value in that he has given me this sweet, five-year-old to guide through all of life's challenges. He has trusted me to love her and to be a representative of His love and grace in her life when her world got turned around and thrown on its side.

Because it's not just me. And it's not just my world.

And it's not just you, either.

Your sadness isn't the only sadness.

I know it feels that way.

I get it.

You and I could have a conversation over coffee one day and trust me, we could go toe to toe over whose story is the saddest.

I used to think that if this happened, I'd probably win.

But after listening to so many other women over the months, here's what I've learned. My story is sad, but it's not the saddest story ever known to man. Someone has it worse. And has had it worse.

And God needs me to get over myself.

To get over my expectations. To get over my lack. To get over my disappointment. So that I can minister to others who have had it worse.

It doesn't mean that my lack and my needs and my disappointments won't ever show up. But it means that when they do, I will put them in perspective.

And I will realize that everyone has them.

And instead of sulking about my lack, I will lean into my provision. And instead of a leaking vessel begging for more at every turn, I will allow God to make me a full vessel so that I can pour into others.

But this can only happen when I lean in. Into my present. Into my now. Even when it's not what I expected.

Even when I wanted something different.

Even when I expected more.

Even when I feel like God blew it.

I will lean in. Into God. Into the pain. Into the disappointment. I will press into the healer. And he will give me what I need.

CHAPTER 6

When you want to fight God

This is going to sound ironic after just having finished the last chapter, so just be prepared.

But this morning, I felt God leading me to intercede. But that's not the ironic part.

The ironic part is that God was leading me to intercede, for marriages.

Ya'll.

Am I the only one who has sometimes wanted to have a knock-down, drag-out fight with the creator of the universe and ask him how he could be so cruel?

God, you are asking me to pray for marriages, while mine is in a casket, at the morgue, with the funeral less than a few days away?

Really, you have got to be kidding me!

But my kickback didn't stop His urging.

See, he placed this passion in my heart to fight for families. And it breaks my heart that divorce is so common in today's society.

Sure, relationship issues have always been a thing. The caveman didn't stay committed to their wives like we all assume they did, just because at the end of the day, they still lived in the same home.

Yet still, family dysfunction, separation, and dissolution hasn't always been this normal.

Normal where children don't even blink at having to spend weekends in different houses.

Normal where divorce percentages are rising and marriages are not worth fighting for, anymore.

And that breaks my heart.

And as much as I want this book to not just be about breaking families, singleness, and divorce, it's the season I'm in. And this is the book that God is calling me to write.

Maybe, because if you are on the verge of walking away from something fixable, you will read through these pages and choose to fight through the uncomfortable and the hard because family and marriage God's way is worth it.

And so anyway, I prayed, as God urged.

And again, I surrendered.

I surrendered to the pain of fighting for someone else's success in the area of my failure.

But sometimes friends, that's how we come out.

By choosing to believe that there is purpose in every season and in every-single-thing that God gives us.

It's not embarrassment he is developing when he asks you to fight for that thing that may or may not work, it's passion.

And it's passion for his purpose.

Choose to be passionate about the things he's called you to, regardless of what is thrown in front of you.

If he's placed something in you, if he's given you a heart for something, it's for a reason. And you never know how he's going to use that thing in you.

Be willing to look at dead things and see life. Not just in the things. Everyone always wants the Lazarus in their lives to come back to life.

But even when Lazarus is dead and in the tomb, what can still live because Lazarus once lived?

That's the purpose in your pain.

That's the stuff you take from this season and carry into the next.

And that's what you put in your vessel to pour out to others.

It starts from assessing what's left even in the midst of what was lost.

"Be willing to look at dead things and see life."

CHAPTER 7

Acknowledge your empty

I'm an emotional eater and I love sugar.

And that's a terrible combination when you add to it that I have a condition called polycystic ovarian syndrome, (PCOS.)

PCOS is not a friend of carbs or sugar at all. And I know, in general sugar and carbs are not friends to anyone's body. But since I have PCOS, sugar and carbs make my body go bananas. I gain weight quicker than most, and have severe trouble getting it off due to the hormonal imbalance that PCOS causes. And speaking of that hormonal imbalance, if you want to see an already emotional woman with PCOS go bonkers, give her carbs and sugar.

What's more though, is that the type of bonkers she'll be driven to, is unpredictable.

Depending on the day and the hormones that are currently tripping in my body, I will either cry about everything, or punch everyone.

It's serious.

And the extra weight my body is currently carrying as a result of all of that emotional eating, weight gaining, and hormonal jiggling isn't helping my overall health, and I want to a live a long, healthy life.

So, I've been working out 3 or more days every week. I try to do five usually, but I don't always make the cut.

I've been meticulous about journaling and not using food to comfort my feelings.

But one day, I found myself mindlessly dunking some golden lemon Oreos in some milk and popping them into my mouth. They are my favorite treat and I do not deprive myself when I am eating them in moderation. But suddenly, I stopped and asked myself, "Stephanie, are you even hungry?"

I reasoned within myself that I In fact wasn't.

"Then why are you sitting here eating these cookies?" I asked myself.

"I don't know." I thought.

"I feel…I feel…hurt. Well, I'm not sure it's hurt. I just want to cry and I don't know why. I feel empty."

Clue words, there.

"I feel."

More clue words.

"Hurt." And "Empty."

And food was not the answer to those things.

Jesus was.

And no, this is not just another vulnerable chapter to tell you how messed up I am and how much I need Jesus.

I mean, I am. And I do.

But so do you.

Because food may not be your thing.

But what about sex?

Yes, even if you're married.

Sometimes, we use the things that we have access to as an emotional high to fill our empty so that we don't have to be busy feeling our empty.

And yes, the word play is real and on purpose.

Oftentimes, we are filling our empty with things because we want to avoid feeling our empty through the process of healing.

Sex not your thing?

What about alcohol?

Yes, I know, some of us reading this book, we're Christians.

But has a drink or two ever been your go to on high stress days?

We're friends here. And we all have our issues. So, alcohol, drugs, food, sex. Whatever your filler is, no judgement.

And you know what, they may not all have equal detriment, but they all have equal weight when we use them as fillers.

And none of them satisfy what is truly eating away at us.

What about people?

I've been so guilty of this.

I have a therapist, but boy, have I tried to use my friends and family members as therapist, too. I've gone around feeling so empty, carrying a bottomless cup crying, fill me, heal me, make me feel better.

And I'm not talking about an occasional venting session. Those are healthy from time to time and we all need them.

I'm talking about a consistent moaning session where I try to get someone else to empty their cup into mine because I feel empty.

And emptiness can only be truly filled by God.

In seasons where we are reaching for comfort from things, we need to learn how to reach for his presence.

Not just one time.

But every time.

Every time we are feeling like what we have is not enough.

Every time we are feeling like we are not enough.

Every time we feel like we are failures.

Every time we are feeling that we are forgotten.

We need to run to him, not people.

We need to run to him, and not things.

And if it's encouragement we need, he'll send it.

If it's people we need, he'll send them.

Trust me, I know.

I spent seasons begging for love and people that never showed.

And then I learned to go to God and let him fill me. And I told him what I needed, and he sent it. It seemed like what was in lack when I begged people is now in abundance because I asked God.

So, let my experience be a lesson for you.

Run to God.

Go to God.

Ask God.

Reach for God.

He'll reach for you.

And he'll send you what you need.

CHAPTER 8

Free yourself

Trust me. Nobody gets it more than I do.

The feeling of lonely. Desperately wanting to fit in. Constantly feeling like something is wrong with you.

Eventually, the pain and ache of it all drives you to a place of desperation. And desperation leads you to do anything just so you'll be accepted.

Compromise my values? Sure.

Shrink myself? Sure.

Go with the flow rather than share my opinion? Sure.

I'm so familiar with that in fact that I probably shouldn't be the girl writing this chapter. I'm still finding my way back.

And that is in fact why I thought that maybe I should write this chapter.

Because I know what's it's like to be that woman. That person. And I also know what's it's like to let desperation change you into so many forms and shrink down to so small of a size that you don't even know who you are anymore.

So, I get to be the woman who writes this chapter and screams to you, "Do not do it!"

Do not let desperation shrink you or change you.

You are you for a purpose.

And the people that God has placed in your life, the people that he will bring to your life, the people that he will connect you to in life will like you just for you.

In the middle of a mess and all.

So, friend, get over people.

For real.

Not over them so much that you develop a complex that causes you to square your shoulders and assume that you've got all of life, alone.

But friend, stop screaming for approval.

Stop begging to be liked.

Be okay with who you are.

Be okay whether they call your name or not.

Because those who are called to see you, will see you. And they will love you. And encourage you. And celebrate you.

And those that don't, well… they aren't called to you.

And I know that may be hard to hear. Especially when you've always found yourself on the outside wanting to be apart of the popular crew. Wanting to be known. Wanting to be picked and chosen.

And on the surface, I know that all sounds high schoolish and like we should know this all by now. And maybe some of us do. But I've heard enough stories to know that I'm not the only one trying to shake the people weight.

Because loneliness hurts.

And waiting for God to send the right crew, the right team, the right friends, the right man or woman… it gets old

I know.

When things that come so easily to others seem to take forever to come to you, your middle, your hard, your ache seems deeper and longer.

And it breeds impatience.

And impatience is an open door to desperation.

So, in the waiting and in the middle, we have to remember God.

Remember that we are not alone when we have Him.

And we also need to remember that we are enough with Him.

Because if we're honest, many times, we are alone because we deem ourselves not enough. And so we hide from environments that illuminate our insecurities and we isolate even when God is calling us into community to be known.

So, in actuality, we run from the answer God is calling us to, and into desperation which keeps us from his very best.

Listen, beautiful soul. You are enough. You are wanted. And you are loved.

And you need to know this.

Because if you never know this to be true. I mean really know this to be true, you will rob the world of the gift that is uniquely you, trying to fit in with everyone else.

And the world needs your touch, your love, your smile.

And once lost, it's so very hard to get back.

I don't know when it happened to me. I'm not sure if it happened in school. Or in church as a kid. Or maybe in college when I first realized the world wasn't as small as I imagined. Or in a relationship where I was belittled and started feeling like I had to change myself to be like the women the guy I was with fantasized about, but I lost myself.

And that's hard and scary to admit.

That I didn't realize my value. That I didn't realize that people who didn't want me and couldn't see me didn't deserve me and weren't for me.

It's a painful realization.

And I don't just mean romantically. Platonically, too.

People who care more about aesthetics than character. Or popularity than authenticity. I don't mean to devalue them. We are all on our own journeys.

But as it relates to you, my friend, and to me, they weren't quality people.

And their walking away from what it was we had to offer, was protection.

I know in the middle it doesn't seem like this. I get it. In the middle, all you can see is pain and all you can feel is rejected, but listen, God has so much better in store for you.

And you need to know it, because we cannot afford to wait on you to keep getting your heart together from the rejection that was actually a blessing.

And what's more is that you cannot afford to wait on you either.

Can I tell you something?

You are wasting your time.

Yes, heartbreak comes. And we have to deal and heal.

"Extended time in the dungeon is wasted time outside of the field of Gods purpose, promise, and provision."

But extended time in the dungeon is wasted time outside of the field of Gods purpose, promise, and provision.

You are missing great agonizing over the poor.

And I need you to witness great. So that you can pour out the great. And so that we can experience the great that God has poured into you.

So, friend, get over people. Walk out of shame. Hold you head up high.

You are not what you've been through. And you are not who left you. You are you. And you are incredible.

So maybe today, even in this middle, you can come to this truth and realization. God has something great for you. He's placed something great in you.

He has great people awaiting to surround you.

He just needs you to be willing to let go of the wrong ones.

And trust him enough to walk into your purpose even when you feel abandoned and alone.

CHAPTER 9

Consistency in the inconsistent

Everything was changing for me all at once.

Everything including my professional career.

Having just a few years ago reached a place professionally that I never expected I would be in, life had determined that I start all over again.

From the bottom.

And so, there I was.

In the middle of a major family and dwelling change, also breaking myself into a career change.

Starting from a position I held over twenty years ago, when I found myself just getting a start in corporate America.

Talk about humble beginnings.

Humble start overs is more like it.

I found myself looking around at everything I had and thinking, "This is exactly what things looked like my sophomore year in college. Goodness things have regressed for me."

But the only way to move forward was to accept where I was starting.

At the beginning.

So, I started my new job.

I'm a hard worker.

It's what I do.

But as I started this new job, I couldn't help but find myself a little bewildered, overwhelmed, and stressed.

Training was awesome, but the real work was a very different feel.

I hadn't gotten feedback on my performance for months. And when I had the chance to ask how I was doing and what was expected of me during that period, the feedback I received from upper management was "We don't have very many expectations for you right now."

Yes. For real.

But I took good notes in training.

And every work day, I showed up committed to perform like expectations had already been set in place. I showed up as if I was expected to perform at the top even though their expectations of me at the time, were minimal.

And you know what, I made mistakes.

A bunch of them.

But somehow, amongst my peers, I was still one of the highest performers.

Little did I know that very soon, the company I was working for would lose their contract with the provider I had been assigned to, and that the provider would actually be looking to interview associates that were currently doing the job.

I was new. And I was told that it was unlikely I would be pulled for the job.

But I was.

I was one of the very few from my hired group to actually be offered a job working for the contractor themselves.

And again, transition and uncertainty was a thing.

Although expectations were a little clearer, things were a lot different from the company I was working for before, and I was totally uncertain that I would meet the mark at this new company. And for a while, I had no one to voice my concerns to., until my first meeting with a supervisor.

She threw up some numbers on the board and told me where I was performing in comparison to other long-time associates. I was down at the bottom.

But she told me not to worry.

"I watch your work." She said. "And you are just getting to know these requirements."

"But you are good. And I want you to focus on these things because I want to be able to showcase your work."

I felt confident being able to work with her. And I felt confident in my work.

Until I came in to work one morning and all-of-a-sudden, everything was different.

And I mean everything.

My supervisor was different. My daily schedule was different. Meeting formats were different.

Everything.

I got so may emails and schedules changes one day, my head spun.

But I had learned something from the previous chaos.

And that is that chaos around me doesn't have to cause chaos in me. And even when I am unsure of what is happening around me, my intentional focus on doing right and moving forward shines through the most uncertain circumstances.

And this isn't just true in a work instance, it's true in any circumstance.

Chaos around you doesn't have to mean chaos in you.

You can choose to focus on doing right in circumstances that seem so incredibly wrong.

You can choose to excel and produce even in situations when there is very little being requested and required of you.

You can choose to act as if the support you need is already in place even if you feel wobbly and uncertain in life, in purpose, and in plans.

So, here's what I need you to do. Immediately, as a matter of fact.

Stop staring at your life trying to figure out what happens next. Stop trying to tie every single thing you do to one specific outcome and be persistent and consistent about being your best and doing your best.

That's all.

Even if you are looking at a bunch of rubble around you, you only have one task.

Do your best and be your best.

"Chaos around you doesn't have to mean chaos in you."

CHAPTER 10

Step by Step

I had been expecting it.

The emotional crash.

The holidays weren't just approaching. They were here.

Thanksgiving was just two days away.

And me, well… I was just two events away. From losing it all.

The woman who walked around trying to plaster a smile on her face wasn't real. And although I really wanted her to be, I was starting to realize that she was steady burying the real me. The me who so desperately wanted to be healed and free. And whole.

Because that person was hurting. But she had been hurt by so many people she trusted before. So, she was scared to trust. And uncertain who to trust.

It's not like she never came out.

She felt free to be herself in support groups and classes for self-care. But when those groups were over, she lacked freedom in her real life.

And that girl, was afraid.

So, the girl with the smile painted over her showed up. The girl who was hurting but had to be strong for her daughter, she showed up.

The girl who was hurting, but was scared to be honest in fear of losing the things that mattered most to her, yes, that was the girl who showed up.

But that girl wasn't real.

And the real girl was hurting. And the holiday season was the magnifying glass to her heart that said, "You are not okay."

"You feel broken"

"You feel lost."

"You feel scared."

"And you need to give yourself a voice."

And that voice looked like a slow rise from bed in the mornings.

It looked like a twenty-minute cry before leaving my room.

It looked like an extra weight pulling me back when I shifted about my house trying to get what I needed to get done, done.

But I survived it. Step by step.

And sometimes, that's how it is.

A step by step progression of the day.

Sometimes, we're not all there when pain hits us.

Sometimes, we can't get up in the morning with a skip in our step determined to conquer the day.

Sometimes, we get up instead, with a determination to make it through the day.

And that's okay.

A step-by-step pace doesn't mean that we are sinking into the depths of depression.

It just means that we are slowing down to a pace that allows us to take care of the person in us that is wreaking from pain and disappointment in the midst of being stuck in the middle.

Of whatever.

Maybe, relational changes.

Or maybe death.

Maybe career changes.

Or maybe homelessness.

Whatever the reason, when life calls us to slow our pace, it is not only helpful to listen, it is wise.

Because we can't heal the person that we keep stuffing inside until we let them out.

After all, if the girl or boy who is lost, never admits that they are lost, how will they know what they need is to ask God for guidance?

If the girl or boy who feels let down by God, never knows that they feel let down, how will they know that what they need is to renew their faith and trust?

If the girl or boy who is hiding because they fear rejection, never comes out enough to know that they are hiding, how will they know to ask God to make them perfect again in his love?

We need to listen to the girl and the boy.

We need to slow down for them.

We need to let them speak.

And yes, I referred to voices of our inner wounds as "the girl" and "the boy" because when we are hurting and in pain, it's very often our childlike selves that are crying before God and asking Him for answers.

And it is amazing that in his presence, we can be old and gray, and still run to him as but a child.

And when life just seems to be going too fast, we need to take a moment to go step by step by step.

Because part of getting through the middle is acknowledging that you, are in the middle.

CHAPTER 11

Loss in the Middle

This part. This Chapter. This is the one where I get completely honest. The one where I finally decide to stop saying that this isn't a book about the divorce that I am going through and how it has left me in a rough, sticky, messy middle.

Because it's impossible to encourage you to speak and live in your truth when I am denying mine. So, today, I came to one of my writing spots determined to intentionally stop talking around the monkey, and address it, instead.

And no, I do not mean the monkey, as in my soon to be ex-husband.

Somehow, breakups, whether in relationships or in marriage, they can turn us into ugly people. People who act as if there was never anything that drew two people together in the first place.

The truth is, I loved my husband. Still do. And although feelings of romantic love no longer exist, there will be memories of times we shared and times we met that may fade, but never disappear.

You know, the other day, I heard a very well-known preacher say that life very rarely turns out the way we want it to. And that is so very true. There are people we meet and plan to have in our lives forever that don't stay. Each of us is on our own life's journey. And although in marriage, one would hope that two people are taking the same journey together, sometimes, trauma and tragedy from one's past, and even one's present, gives room to so many spiritual influences. And without a strong internal persuasion, outside accountability and support, these influences can be very easy for one to succumb to.

And so, the two, walk as two, in two different directions.

And it is painful.

And today, my heart hurts.

More than I imagined it could ever hurt again.

More than I care to allow it. But it hurts, still.

The breaking, the tearing, the questions, the sadness, the anger, the frustration, the fear. It's all real. It's all intense. Sometimes, seemingly all coming at me at once. Sometimes, giving me a chance to breathe in between, as waves of grief overtake me.

Sometimes, I feel like God is with me. Holding me through the pain. Other times, I feel forsaken, unable to breathe, and like I will collapse under the weight. My journal pages look like someone bipolar wrote them.

One day, I feel like God is with me and I'm praising Him for moving mountains and smoothing out valleys.

Other days, I feel forsaken. Like he doesn't have me at all. Like he is attending to everyone else and their needs, except mine.

It's a roller coaster of emotions.

Divorce. I get it. Sometimes, it's necessary. Sometimes, it's unavoidable because you are fighting alone. Or with someone who is addicted or abusive. I get it.

But my God, I don't understand how anyone in their right mind chooses this without absolute reason.

We have a five-year old daughter.

And while I won't write what I think to be her internal story for all to see before she is able to put her own story into words, what I will say, is that it's confusing, scary, and heartbreaking.

The very first time she told me that us not all living together broke her heart, it broke mine.

And again, I don't understand how anyone in their right mind chooses this without absolute reason.

But there comes a point when whether or not this is what I chose for my life, or this is what life chose for me, no longer matters. This is what it is.

And so, reality looks a lot like processing very, very difficult questions and realities.

How could someone I fought so hard for leave me so easily? Why didn't they see my value? Why didn't they care enough about me to make it work? How could anyone else ever come in the middle and eradicate all of the history we have together? All of the memories and all of the love?

Hard questions. Real questions.

It's weird, you know?

I cried on Thanksgiving morning, the first year I knew we were divorcing.

I spent it with some friends of mine. And when I heard her and her husband in the kitchen, up early in the morning laughing and talking, something in me was happy for them and the love they shared but sad for me at the same time.

The hard times had been so hard that very few people know that it wasn't always hard.

The guy who was leaving me now had also been the guy that made me smile on many days. He was the guy that I spent the most time feeling like a kid with. He was the guy that tickled me in bed and the guy that I had pillow fights with.

And so, I was sad for me because I remembered those sounds.

But the sadness I felt only made me want to encourage my friends to never let that sound go.

By gosh, I don't care how hard it gets, and marriage does get hard. But don't give that up. Don't let that go. That laughter. Those early morning sounds in the kitchen with just you and him when the kids are still sleep and there is no one else around. You may not always agree, but always remember moments in the kitchen that drive you to love, that drive you to smile, that drive you to laugh at things only the two of you know about.

Always, remember.

And so, I cried. I cried for the love that I had that I no longer had, not in that way.

And I guess I'm writing this because no one really shares what it is really like to have your heart ripped into shreds and a family torn apart.

Not that I've heard. Not that I've read.

Not with honesty that still covers. And truth that shares the painful moments with a gentle sliver of hope.

Marriage is beautiful.

My marriage was beautiful.

It hasn't ended that way. There have been hurtful words. Spoke by us both. There has been realization on my part of how little I was valued. There has been complete disregard. There has been recognizing and realizing that the person I first loved and fell in love with no longer exists. And I'm sure that he feels that way, too.

Marriage. When it ends, it's painful.

And in the middle, most days, my feelings can be summed up in one word. Devastation.

My questions, unending.

My fears, unrelenting.

I wonder if I'll ever find happy again. I wonder if I'll ever experience love again. I wonder if the breaking of my marriage will somehow break my child in all the ways I tried my hardest to prevent.

And so, I'm in my middle, feeling lost. Feeling scared. Feeling uneasy.

And having no choice but to trust God.

And as much as that sounds like a great option to be left with, it's also a scary option to be left with.

Because who knows the mind of God?

Who knows what he is going to do next? Or where he is going to turn next?

And my heart, in the middle of this, feels like it's at its weakest. And I'm not sure I can take another one of God's turns.

And yes, I know the next turn could be a great one. But the unknown is scary.

And so, when I feel uneasy and overcome with emotion, I am learning to stop for a minute and filter my uncertainty through the lens of his love.

If he has allowed for me to be here in this moment, he has a plan for this season, this space, and this place.

He is using this to work something for my good and for the good of others.

He is not a God that sees me with eyes of hate and disdain, but lavish love.

> "If he has allowed for me to be here in this moment, he has a plan for this season, this space, and this place."

The pain I feel now is because his love wants better for me.

And so, I surrender to what hurts now to have what is best later.

I have a God who loves me.

And you have a God who loves you, too.

Because, we all have hard things.

Things that leave us with questions.

Things that leave us with pain that feels beyond unbearable.

Things that make us question the goodness of God.

Things that leave us feeling like we have to brace ourselves before we decide to trust God fully, because who knows what He's going to do next.

But friends, he loves us.

And whatever pain He allows now is because he has something better in store for us then.

So, in this chapter, and in your middle, will you join me in trusting him through the very messy, hard, and painful places?

Will you join me in trusting that now looks nothing like what the end will be?

And I know this last thing will be hard, but will you also join me in believing that this next turn will be a good turn?

I know it's scary. I know we've gotten used to bracing ourselves for the drop.

But the love of God is far too sure to choose to give in to a life of only devastation.

Good things are coming. To you. And to me.

So, let's take a deep breath and believe him for incredible.

CHAPTER 12

Lying Feelings in the Middle

The last time I tried to open my heart, I was hurt.

And hurt is a teacher.

Although sometimes, the way we understand the lessons hurt is trying to teach us, isn't always accurate.

See, in that season of my life, hurt was supposed to teach me that only God could fill the empty places in my heart that I was running around asking people to fill.

And although my head knows that now, my heart feels betrayed and abandoned. And so my heart says, "Protect me and refuse to trust anybody else again."

Refuse to forgive. That way, you win. And that way, the person who tried to punish you by avoiding you, loses.

Hurt is a teacher.

But sometimes, pride won't allow us to learn what we really need to learn.

And so, we pretend to be stronger than we really feel.

We pretend our hearts are more healed than they really are.

And we keep everyone out and at bay.

But helpers out, equals turmoil in. And turmoil in, equals stuck. In. The. Middle.

And inviting helpers in starts with being honest about what's going on in the heart.

For me, this is what happened on a Sunday morning, when I showed up to church unable to keep up the charade.

I was worshipping a God that I was pretending not to be mad at.

And although my worship was real and not just a public display, my heart and my questions were rising to the surface.

I loved him, but I was mad at him.

I wanted to trust him, but I was disappointed by him.

I wanted to sing about his goodness, but I didn't understand how his goodness would have allowed the situation I was in. And I couldn't do it.

I couldn't keep singing about Jesus without first addressing the questions in my heart.

I had to stop and say it. I had to stop and address it. I had to stop and ask it.

"God, you're good. I know you are good. But why did you allow this? And why don't I feel like you are good to me?"

In other words, I had to ask him, point blank. "God, if you are so good, then where were you then? And where are you now?"

Ya'll. Have you ever just had a real conversation with God?

If you have, have you ever been scared that he was going to strike you down, afterwards?

I'm always afraid that God will get mad at me for having the audacity to be mad at him.

And then I get scared that he will take away all of the things that I actually do have.

But that always takes me back to the fact that he is good.

He did disappoint me. And he didn't give me what I wanted, but he has been good to me.

And then, my temper tantrum seems pointless.

But here's the thing, my temper tantrum was never really pointless.

Because had I never voiced my disappointment to God, the conviction in my spirit would not have prompted me to remember his goodness. I would've been stuck holding in feelings of disappointment.

The other day, a friend and I were having a conversation and she said something to me that made me mad. But I didn't let her know.

She was encouraging me. And as I told her how difficult I felt my current situation was, she said, "Well, He always brings you out."

And I was angry.

Not angry at her, but angry at that statement. Because I didn't feel out.

I felt like the last eight years of my life had been a season of continual grief and devastation. And every time I tried to peek out, I felt like I kept getting thrown back into the pit.

But I had learned something from a previous season of grief, spouting back everything thing that my injured heart feels when someone attempts to encourage me isn't really a great thing to do.

Instead, when I hear something that pricks my touchy heart, I need to realize that my processor is a little off and at the very least, realize that the person on the other end of the phone, or of a conversation, isn't only just trying to encourage me, but they also have a different perspective.

And so, when my friend and I finished our conversation, instead of being offended, I decided to pray and ask God to show me ways that he had in fact brought me out.

And although I still didn't feel out of any of those seasons, I was able to list signs of provisions, waves of grace, and paths of direction.

And so, I took a breath and realized God was with me, then. And he was with me now.

I was angry, but I was honest.

And the lies of my feelings were exposed and covered by the truth of his love.

"The lies of my feelings were exposed and covered by the truth of his love."

CHAPTER 13

It's not real. but it hurts.

I wouldn't tell my daughter a single thing.

And she was sitting in the backseat pouting our entire car ride.

She wanted to know where we were going.

And I wanted it to be a surprise.

I had been planning it for the whole week.

I knew she'd be excited.

But I didn't want her to know where we were going until we got there, so the whole time, she was upset because she felt like I was being mean to her by not answering her questions.

Inquisitive is not an adequate enough word to describe her personality. She absolutely does not like to be left in the dark.

But if she knew, it would've ruined the journey there.

And so, she pouted. She pouted as we walked into familiar surrounding because that only made her more upset.

How could we be in a place she loved but not doing what she wanted? Or at least she thought we wouldn't be doing what she wanted.

I tried to keep her distracted the entire time until we walked into the door.

It was a movie she had been wanting to see for the longest time.

She was so excited that she literally screamed in theatre.

And I then turned to her and said, "Now who's the best mom in the world?"

"You are! She said with the biggest smile expression she could muster up.

All that time, she thought she was being denied. And it hurt her. It made her angry. It made her pout.

And all that time, I was preparing her for the excitement of something she really wanted.

You see where I'm going, don't you?

Well, I'm glad you do.

Because in these next few Chapters, we are leaving the pit of despair and stepping into the light of truth.

And here's the kicker.

At the end of this book, we'll still all probably be stuck in the middle of something.

Because a revelation of truth doesn't always immediately lead us to a destination.

But it does help us to start back to walking towards a destination.

Because the only way to get out of a messy middle is to wade through the mess, right?

So, let's talk about it.

The mess of our feelings and how they often lead us away from truth.

Is God really withholding His good from us?

Or is just that our feelings are in the blind spot of His love?

His preparation of the great things He has in store for us often requires leaving us in the dark, all the while asking us to trust His plan.

And blindly trusting in the middle is not easy.

But it is what He ask of us.

As the good parent.

To trust that He is good and that where He is leading us is good.

What if my daughter would have rode in the car with great anticipation instead of great agitation?

How much better might that car ride have been for her if she thought to herself, "My mommy loves me. And if she isn't telling me where we are going, it's got to be somewhere exciting for me!?"

In reality, the ride might not have felt so long for either of us.

In my humanness, her pouting almost triggered me to turn the car around and change the destination altogether.

Praise God, He is not like us.

He is patient with us, even when we pout about being in the dark.

Even when we start looking for clues.

Even when we start planning an alternate journey and destination for ourselves because His trip is taking too long.

He is patient.

But if we trust well, and if we expect that His outcome will only be to our benefit, then how much more peace and joy will we have on our journey as we trust Him?

So, trust him, friends.

Being left in the dark only hurts when we forget the intentions of our Father.

And then, our hurt, it really hurts.

But our hurt isn't based on a real perception of God and what He is doing in our lives.

And how awful to waste painful emotions on a journey to a joyous destination.

CHAPTER 14

Mark the moment,

I wasn't having a very joyous time at all looking at my finances one day. It was on the 2nd of August and I had paid all of my major bills and taken my daughter school shopping, and the amount sitting in my account until my next payday made me want to cry.

I looked at that amount in disgust. "This is all I have?" I thought to myself. All my hard work and I'm left with only this?"

And then I looked at the number again.

And it was almost as if God spoke to me in the voice of my natural father that day. Because I could hear my earthly dad very clearly in my head.

I didn't even realize that instead of being disgusted in the moment, I should've in fact been dancing and praising.

Because the amount that I was disgusted about, used to be all I had, not just all I had left.

The amount in my bank account that I had left after paying my bills in this moment, used to be the exact amount that I had in my paycheck to try to figure out how to pay all the major bills that I had just paid. After all, it wasn't that long ago that I couldn't even afford to take my daughter school shopping. A friend had to help do that for me. And now, here I was, having paid bills, taken my daughter shopping, and put groceries in my fridge, having the audacity to be mad that an entire once upon a time pay check was all I had left in my account.

And immediately, my attitude of lack and disdain shifted to "God, you are amazing! I just paid all of my bills and I have a whole paycheck left! Look what you have done!"

See, in the middle of a mess, we sometimes don't even pay attention to all the miracles happening along the way.

We don't realize how what once was our struggle, is now our portion.

And we miss the moment.

See, moments like these are meant to be journaled and kept. Not just on paper, but in our hearts.

They are meant to be marked as pillars of God's faithfulness and promise along the way of our path.

So, mark the moment.

Jot down the testimonies of God's faithfulness and hold them near.

Because we are often so focused on the messy that we seldom sit in awe at the ways made in the mess.

CHAPTER 15

Call it what it really is

Depression has been attaching itself to me ever since I can remember.

From struggling with the effects of being a child of divorce, to the death of my three-year-old daughter when I was only 27 years of age, to a very traumatic divorce after thirteen years of marriage, life has definitely not been a crystal stair for me.

So, depression has tried to make itself my friend more times than I can count.

And so, when I found myself having to grieve a friendship with one of my closest friends, I knew for sure my old friend, depression, was coming along for the ride.

I did what I knew to do to keep my old friend, depression, at bay, but I knew it, just like before, there it was.

"I'm sad," I thought to myself.

And then I said it out loud.

But then, I immediately started to assess the situation.

I was grieving the loss of something I held dear. Or the potential loss of something I held dear. Because right now, that story is still in its middle, too.

So, I'm not going to put a period on that sentence just because it's a chapter in this book.

But for now, yes, it feels like death, and so I am grieving.

Yes, even while writing this Chapter.

That's my real.

And let's be honest, my real is probably the reason why you are still reading this book, because when you are in the middle, expert advice from someone who seems to be on their mountain top just doesn't cut it.

It seems unrelatable.

As if you are drowning in a sorrowful situation and they are rejoicing from the mountains trying to tell you all the reasons why you should be happy.

Yes, I get it.

I know.

I've been there, too.

And so, I've chosen to purposely write to you while I am grieving, but reaching.

So we're not going to have the begrudging conversation about our sorrowful pit today, but I'm also not going to give you a list of reasons why you should be grateful and put a smile on your face either.

Grief is hard.

Loss is hard.

Uncertainty is hard.

But, to try to beat depression at its offset, I did some things.

I put myself on a social media break.

I temporarily shut down all of my social media accounts for 60 days with the exception of Instagram.

Instagram wasn't a place I went very often, and it didn't cause me to compare or dwell on the lives of others very much.

So, I kept that one account open.

But I restricted myself from posting anything for two weeks.

This was a rule I made for myself in order to force me to process my emotions through journaling, instead of prematurely using my pain to encourage others.

See, it is easy to hide behind a gift or a calling, when it encourages others, as a means of escape from processing personal pain.

But this is not true healing.

So, I put a pause on external ministry even, so that I could focus on allowing God to heal the brokenness of my own heart.

And so, I assessed what I was feeling in the moment.

Yes, I was sad.

But sadness wasn't the overarching feeling in that moment.

I was just bored.

Depending on when you are picking up this book and reading it, you may or may not be familiar with the events of 2020-2021.

But, if you are not, just look up Covid 19.

I was locked up in a house with my eight-year-old daughter (yes, some time has passed since I've picked my pen back up) and I had shut down all social media.

That day, I had been to the gym, taken my daughter to the mall and out to lunch, and then I drove around trying to think of groups I could attend, places I could volunteer or somewhere I could go, but...nadda.

The world was shut down.

I mean, semi-open.

But this was around the time where the delta variant of Covid was ramping up and numbers were rising again.

And so, just as I was hopeful that groups would start opening again - - - nope!

And so, I was home. In a house that needed to be cleaned.

But I didn't have the motivation for that just yet.

So, I called this feeling that I was feeling sadness.

But really, it was boredom.

And it was important for me to name the feeling what it really was to recognize the state that I was in.

I may have been sad.

But I wasn't overtaken by depression.

And that was a victory.

And because I named the feeling correctly, I could address the feeling.

I had been spending so much time surfing the internet looking at other people's lives, that I hadn't realized how empty my life really was.

Not empty in a hollow, woe is me, way.

But empty of things that I could and even possibly should have been doing to move my own life forward.

My life was void of creativity because I was spending so much time mindlessly surfing.

And don't get me wrong, social media has its place.

I love it.

But when I named the feeling of boredom, I realized how much of a place I had given social media in my life, when it was only supposed to have a small space.

We cannot assess what we never address.

And if we are not careful to accurately name a thing, we can very often mistake God's presence for his absence, and his invitation for his abandonment.

Is the space in your life that you keep naming as a familiar ailment actually now a healed place?

And is the emptiness you're rushing to fill with trivial things, actually God's invitation for you to produce?

Assess so you can address.

Name it what it really is.

CHAPTER 16

A Friend In The Middle

I didn't want to say anything out loud, but I had wondered why a co-worker had chosen to take a full eight weeks off of work for a leg injury when we all worked from home.

And no, I wasn't judging her.

After all, it was her time to use.

But she was the leader of a brand new team that she seemed so excited to be a part of, so I just didn't get the reason for her extended absence.

I knew she had experienced an injury. And I knew that she had to have surgery and that there would be a long recovery period, but from what I had learned of her and about her, it seemed more probable that she would prop her leg up on something of comfort, take some pain medication and do what she could to be at work for a small part of the day at least.

And my presumptions were based upon her go-getter attitude more than an expectation of her return to work.

Her extended absence just didn't seem like her.

It wasn't until after she returned to work that I understood it all.

When we spoke for the first time after her return to work, she preceeded our conversation with, "Technically, I could've come back to work a long time ago, since I'm at home and really just needed to prop my leg up on something. But I was getting so frustrated with all of the things that I couldn't do for myself, and I couldn't come back to work and lead a team when I was feeling that bitter."

And I got it.

We talked a while longer.

And she continued to tell me how her boyfriend and her mom were troopers through it all and helped her a great deal.

She couldn't have gotten through what she did, without them.

But I imagine that there were times that she wasn't so pleasant to deal with during those times that she was feeling bitter about her inability to do the things she once could.

And it takes a special gentleness from those we love to walk with us when our hearts are hurting.

When we are in the middle of recovery.

When our words aren't so sweet and our demeanor isn't always so friendly.

Friends who love us through our messy places are absolute treasures.

And although I'm sure we probably do thank them for the role that they play in our lives, I'm not sure that they get enough credence for the assignment that they fulfill for us.

And yes, I said assignment.

Because even though friendship is voluntary, I believe that one has to be specifically assigned to walk with someone closely and intimately through the messy middle places of their lives.

Because it is not easy.

Often, as a friend, we have a single default when we see our friends hurting.

We try to fix it.

And maybe we can't fix it with our actions, but when we can't physically do anything about it, we try to fix it in our heads, so we offer advice.

Because surely if they do this thing or that thing, or if they hadn't done that thing or the other thing, this would all be different.

So, yeah.

We throw our unsolicited opinions at them, which oftentimes, only makes them feel worse.

Because most things in the messy middle of life cannot be fixed.

My co-worker had torn a ligament in her leg and had to endure surgery.

And now, all of a sudden, the things that she could do just weeks before, she could no longer do.

And some things, she wouldn't be able to do again for at least a year.

There is no advising that away.

Likewise, the mental pain and anguish that one feels and endures from sicknesses and losses and hurts, cannot be advised away.

It cannot be pushed away.

It has to be lived through.

And so, as an assigned friend to someone in their messy middle place, very often, your role is to sit quietly with them in their painful place and share in their pain.

And when it seems as if the pain is becoming unbearable, an assigned friend will remind their friend of who God is in them and who they are in God.

An assigned friend helps gather the pieces for re-build in the time of breakdown.

Because an assigned friend knows that all is not lost, even when a friend going through, feels that all has been lost.

An assigned friend helps gather the pieces for re-
build in the time of breakdown.

And what a blessing and a treasure it is to have a friend who will say, "Friend, I know this pain doesn't belong to me, but because you are my friend, I will sit here in it with you."

Friends are a treasure.

And so, yes, dear assigned friends, I stuck a chapter in this book just for you.

Because in some ways, your friend's messy middle becomes a part of you, too.

So, here's what I need you to know.

Taking care of you is important.

In this season, God may have given us the assignment to pour extra love into our friend who is hurting, but it is impossible to pour from a pitcher that barely has a drop of water in its corner.

It is okay to detach from your friend from time to time to take care of you. Yes, even if they are your assignment.

Here's why.

Because even if they are your assignment, they are also God's assignment.

And so are you.

In their time of need, trust that when you need to go refresh, God will assign others to your friend in need.

And take the time you need to draw from those that God has assigned to refresh you and allow God to refresh you.

Because he never assigns us to others without assigning others to us.

And when we can't find our assigned people, he is a well of refreshment that does not run dry.

And then when you are full, you can get back on your post and minister to your friend.

But sometimes, even with a full heart and the purest of intention, being a friend to someone in the messy middle gets difficult.

It's hard to know what to say, how to say it, if you should say it, and when to say it.

And so, I thought I would share two of my best friend moments that ministered so much healing to me when I needed it most while in my messy middle.

It's through the trial and error of friendship and building friendship that myself and my circle of friends have learned to be friends to each other during difficult seasons and messy middles.

The first story I will tell you is about a time I was feeling particularly devasted. And I mean, devastated.

I wasn't suicidal, but I do remember sitting across the couch from my friend on the couch in my living room and asking why in the year 2020 when so many people had gotten sick and died from Covid, that I was still left here on earth to deal with so much emotional pain.

And so no, I wasn't going to take my life, but I was angry that I still had life.

And my friend, just sat there.

After a while, the conversation had gotten too heavy for even me to bear in the moment, and so I asked my friend if we could get out.

We decided that we would stroll through Target.

But while strolling through Target, I was still an emotional wreck.

And I kept walking off down aisles away from my friend because I didn't want her to see me that angry and that hurt.

I was also afraid that she would regret ever coming to see me in the first place, because in the moment, it appeared that her presence wasn't helping and she could've been doing something more productive with her time.

But instead, she was with me.

And you know what? She stayed with me.

She found me in her own time down every aisle I escaped to.

And when we had left the store and gotten back to my house, she gave me the longest hug before she left.

She hadn't talked much at all that day while we were together. But before she released her grip on that hug, she said these words "I'm sorry. I don't know what to say. But I figured I would just be here."

The love I felt from my friend in that moment.

She didn't tell me that I was an awful friend.

She didn't tell me that I had an awful attitude or list all of the sacrifices she made for me on that day.

She just wanted to be there for me.

And that meant the world.

So, here's my first note to help your through friendship in the messy middle.

When your friend is going through, don't try to fix what you cannot fix.

Don't try to comfort when you know that words will not do.

Just be there.

In their anger.

In their hurt.

Trail slowly behind when they try to escape in shame.

Hug them tight when they will let you.

And just be there.

Here's helping word two. Speak slowly.

This word came from an experience I had with a friend and co-worker.

We worked together as leaders and coaches for a new hire team, and so it was our norm to meet at the beginning of the day to game plan.

During that time, we would usually do a brief check on everyone in the leadership team to get a reading on their personal state as well.

And in our meeting, I happened to share that although I was present and able to work as if I was fine, that on a personal level, I was in fact not fine and having a difficult time.

Having heard that, my friend asked if I needed to take some time to talk after our professional meeting.

I took her up on the offer and reached out to her via video chat after our team meeting.

She answered my call via video chat and immediately turned on her camera to show that she was fully present.

I started by asking her about her morning first.

But once she shared, and then asked me about me, I found myself crying for a good solid five minutes straight as I explained what I was feeling and going through that day.

Quiet, fast tears just kept falling uncontrollably out the side of my eyes.

And once I finished my whole spill, I apologized for offloading it all on her.

That's one of my insecure traits – feeling unworthy of being heard the way that I hear others. I'm working on that.

I threw that side note in there for anyone else who needed to work on that as well. But back to the story I was sharing, once I finished offloading to my friend, she stopped.

She paused.

She made a statement.

And then she asked a question.

And it sounded like this.

"I'm here for you. Did you just want to talk? Or can I say something?"

Friendship.

It asks, "What do YOU need?"

Because friendship is support.

It's not a construction site.

We are not fixing each other.

We are loving, comforting, and supporting each other.

And so, I thanked my friend for having the consideration enough to ask the question, and shared with her that I would like to hear her thoughts.

But before she shared anything from her perspective, she acknowledged the aspects of my life that she could only sympathize with because she had not experienced them, or even had the understanding or wherewithal to know what it might be to go through them.

And that again, was validating the safety of our friendship.

It was her saying, "Hey, I'm here for you and I want to be here for you, but I get that I don't know how you feel or what you're going through."

So, speak slowly.

Ask what they need.

And understand and be okay with the things that you do not understand.

And oh, friend, one last thing before we end this chapter.

I know I keep calling this an assignment.

But I also keep calling this friendship.

What I need you to know is that you matter, too.

Pure assignments may be a one-way street.

But friendship is a two-way street.

Yes, your friend may be in a bitter place.

But what you are not is a consistent punching bag or unending source of advice and encouragement given with no return.

I am a firm believer that friends check each other.

So, know that even in the messiest of middles, your gift of friendship is to be valued.

You are a treasure.

And to my treasured friends, and on the behalf of your treasured friends, thank you for being a friend.

CHAPTER 17

The Messy We Create

The kitchen wasn't spic and span, but it was decent.

The counters had been wiped down.

The dishes were done.

And the floors had been swept.

But the dishes in the dish rack were towered far above the rim.

And the counters, although wiped down, were cluttered with clean dishes that had yet to be put up.

I intended to put the dishes up at some point during the day, but in the immediate moment, my focus was on filling my gallon jug with ice and water.

And so, I pulled the ice container out of my fridge, sat it on the counter, and began to fill my jug with ice and water.

And just as I was getting ready to put my ice tray back in the freezer, I mistakenly knocked over my jug filled with water and ice, that in turn spilt onto the counter where the clean dishes were sitting, and soaked some recipe cards that were stacked nearby.

What a mess I was left to clean up.

Frustrated with myself and the situation, I started aggressively grabbing dishes and throwing them into the sink.

One dish hit another in the drying rack and the tower of dishes in the rack also began to tumble down.

What a nightmarish mess I had created simply by trying to put some water in a jug.

Or, was it putting water in the jug that was the issue? Or was it the fact that I hadn't taken the time to put up what needed to be put up first, that was the issue?

After all, if I hadn't had to squeeze my jug and ice container in such a small space in the first place, what's the probability that I would've hit it with my elbow?

And had I put the dishes up that were sitting on the counter, had the water spilt, I would not have had to re-rinse and dry dishes.

And had I not had the dishes still towering in the rack, when the dishes were sitting on the counter, and had to be placed in the sink, would they have hit the dishes in the rack and caused them to tower over?

Of course, I know that you get it.

And I also know that this scenario is more normal in most of our kitchens than we'd like to admit.

This chapter isn't about making you feel guilty for not having a perfectly clean and put away kitchen.

But it is a call to accountability and responsibility.

To take notice of the messes we create for ourselves in our messy middle.

Because in the middle of a mess, impatience, irritation, and frustration sneak in.

And instead of waiting out the middle, we can become antsy in our own eagerness to get to what we want that we reach for our empty jugs to fill with whatever we are thirsty for, accidently tip them over, and create a larger mess in the middle of our mess.

It's hard, I know.

Sitting in the middle of a mess and taking small steps with God to clean it up.

But the mess we can create when we don't take the small steps and wait it out can be much more damaging.

I've done this a time or two.

Gotten impatient.

Taken an action before time.

And had to sit in time out when my choices didn't pan out the way I had hoped they would.

My heart was torn when I mishandled a friendship.

And although it wasn't just my mishandling that caused it to break apart into a wide-open mess, I spent a lot of time ruminating on my missteps and mistakes.

There were things I knew I should've handled differently.

And because I ran too fast to grab the jug of my longing and fill it up with the wrong type of friendship before its time, there I sat with my aching heart.

And to add insult to injury, I had come so far in healing my heart just prior to, but this ache felt worse than the initial heartache which one would have assumed would hurt greater.

Oh, my aching heart.

But I had to admit something to myself.

I did that.

It wasn't God.

And it wasn't even life.

It was me.

My choice.

My impatience.

My overstepping.

And I had messed it up so extensively, that something I did feel was meant to be in some way, I wasn't sure it would ever quite be fixable again.

And so, I prayed.

God, I messed that up.

But I desperately want another chance.

Amen.

And then, as I waited on his answer, I had to begin cleaning what I messed up.

I had to return to the beginning of my healing process.

And from the beginning, God and I started to clean up the mess that I had made.

And yet, in that sentence, I find great relief.

That God will not leave me alone to clean the messes that even I have made,

That the grace of God is so immeasurable that even when you mess it up, He'll help you clean it up.

Because He walks with us even in the middle of a mess we created.

CHAPTER 18

Hope in the Middle of the Mess

We had a fight. A friend fight, as my daughter would call it. A huge one.

And somehow, I knew that there was no coming back from this.

We had left words left unsaid far too long.

And then the explosion of all the things we should've talked out before it had gotten to the present point, was now out in the open. And both of us had left each other bleeding in ways that I knew the scarring would be a visible reminder of why we could no longer be the type of friends that we once were.

One fight. And just like that, the person that I had known and called my best friend for the last five years was no longer in my life.

We would talk everyday on most days.

Sometimes, we would talk several times a day.

We went out to lunch frequently.

I considered she and her husband family. Even their pet was family to me.

And I know that to them, I was the same.

See, oftentimes, when things like this happen, we try to label it a right or wrong and pin it on a person.

But sometimes, there is no one right or wrong person.

There was just a situation.

A situation that no matter how unintentional, created a painful parting of ways.

And very few people talk about the loss from losing a best friend.

It was painful.

But in that loss, there was the gift of time.

And in that time, I started to write.

What many people don't know is that I never set out to write to another soul.

I was writing to myself.

Because not only had I lost my best friend, I was also struggling through a failing marriage.

And in trying to wrestle with feelings of loss and abandonment, I needed an outlet to express my feelings.

And to reach for God.

And have Him speak to me.

And by the time I felt that I had written out enough of my heart, I looked up and saw that I had written enough for a book.

And so I went back through what I had written to assess if there was a purpose for the words I had written for myself, that was beyond me.

And thus, my first book was started, Grace in a Shattered Place.

Out of loss, came the birth of a book.

And so, earlier this week, when I found myself fearing the effects of another loss, I stopped to remind myself that the last time a situation of painful loss hit my life, a book was born.

And so, in the middle of my crying, I paused to ask myself a question.

What is the gift that this mess is giving me?

And so, that's the question I'm going to ask you.

But I guess, first, we need to define and identify our own mess.

In the season of life that I just shared with you, the mess was the loss of my best friend.

What is yours?

Getting through grief after the loss of a loved one?

Struggling with anxiety and depression?

Losing a job?

Social isolation in the middle of a pandemic?

A debilitating illness?

A tumultuous divorce?

Fighting to stay through a difficult marriage?

If none of the mentioned scenarios fit your messy, write it down in your own copy of this book.

Because messy is hard.

And in every bit of messy, there is a bit of loss.

Loss of a person. Loss of health. Loss of finances. Loss of normalcy.

And loss is devastating.

And devastation can leave us staring at the losses for far too long.

But even from the losses, there is something to be saved and spared.

A treasure in the ruins.

For me, it was the gift of time and reflection that in turn birthed a book for me to share with others.

What is it for you?

Because mess never leaves us with nothing to hold on to.

Define your loss. Find your gift. And hold on to hope in the middle of the messy.

CHAPTER 19

Rebuild in the middle of messy

I was talking to a co-worker the other day whose dad had recently passed, and she shared a quote that someone had given her that resonated with her loss. "If one part of your life does a titanic, you make a raft and hold on to what's left."

Listen, if I you think I've been real already, just hold on, because this is the part of the book where I really get real.

Not about my emotions, but about my situation.

My messy middle.

If you've been reading along with me from the beginning, you haven't gotten this far without the knowledge that I began writing this book while I was going through a divorce.

I was in no rush to hurry through these chapters to get to an end, because I wanted to make sure that what was released was going to be helpful to each person that picked up this book to read it, and not just an airing out of my own emotions.

And so, I withheld the real of my story until now.

Several years on the other side, I am now able to tell this part of the story without emotion.

But I am not unfamiliar with what it looks like when a titanic hits your life and leaves you with nothing but pieces.

Having recently taken in our now daughter, who was in foster care at the time, my ex-husband and I both agreed that I would leave my full-time job to work a part time job from home, so that I could be there for our daughter.

She had been through some trauma and her behavioral issues were requiring one or both of us to leave our jobs in the middle of the day to deal with an issue she was having at her daycare.

Having already been struggling with extra stress on my job, and the fear that having to leave frequently would cause further issues, we agreed that it would be helpful for our daughter's sake, and for me personally, to leave my full-time job working for the state.

I've often been told that my efforts to cover my ex-husband can also be misconstrued as making excuses for what I was made to go through at the expense of his actions.

But what I know to be true is that sin clouds judgment.

And even when we intend to not maliciously hurt those who have loved us, the enemy has a way of blinding us to external consequences to feed our own desires.

And with that knowledge, I do not defend or excuse the actions of my ex-husband, but I also do not nail him to a cross for what God has forgiven him of and what God has used to give me a greater witness and ministry to share with others.

And so, I share this part of my story with respect for his, but honor for my own.

I had been working part time from home for maybe a month before my ex-spouse had decided for the second time that he no longer wanted to be married and was leaving our family.

We had disagreements, of course. But our home wasn't, and had never been a war zone. We were friends, and the moments we shared together were real.

But the responsibility and sacrifice of being a husband and father were not responsibilities and sacrifices that my ex-husband wanted to make.

To be honest, they weren't sacrifices or responsibilities he ever wanted to have at a time.

He had followed a path he was brought up to take for a long time and felt like he was living a lie.

And so, he decided to do what he felt was right for him, by leaving us.

And although his leaving would have been painful no matter how he chose to do it, there was an extra level of pain and difficulty because of how he chose to do it.

I believe he didn't want to give himself or anyone else time to convince him to do otherwise, so the day that he told me he was leaving was the day he started packing to do so.

It was two to three weeks before my daughter was supposed to start kindergarten.

He had called our landlord without my knowledge and told them that we would not be renewing the lease on our home.

So, with just two weeks notice, I had to find a place to live that I could afford on my part time salary. There was nothing available in my price range near the area we were currently living in, so I would also have to get my child into a new school and registered.

In two weeks.

On a part time salary.

All the while, still processing that my ex-husband had just walked out, and dealing with all of the emotions that came with the breaking up of our family unit.

If you didn't understand already, I'm sure that now you can understand why my anger and disappointment with God were beyond explainable.

I didn't understand how His goodness would allow me to go through such a hardship.

Not only was I going through the loss of a marriage, I had lost the person I had considered to be my best friend, and the person I had spent years of my life going through hardships with. No, there weren't only hardships. There were good times, too.

But here I was, going through the worst of hardships and the person I trusted to be by my side through times like this one, was the very reason I was going through this.

So, all at once. There went my marriage. My friend. My home. My career.

And there I was, feeling like I had lost it all, having to make a choice to rebuild.

And for months at a time, it seemed like I was in freezing waters holding onto a raft.

And my raft was my relationship with God. It was my daughter. And it was the part time job that had cut my recent full time check in almost half.

But I held on to what I had.

I worshipped. I kept being the mom I knew how to be, and when I showed up to work, I worked my entry-level part time job like I was at the top of the company.

Four months later, I was offered a full-time position in the company. Eight months later, I was offered the opportunity to obtain a certification that would allow me to promoted to a higher position in the company. I studied for the certification, passed the test, and was offered a higher position three months later, and then three months from that, I was offered a leadership position in my company that advanced my salary beyond what I had ever made at any point in my married life.

God blew my mind.

But it wasn't just about the money.

It was about the life that was coming together around me with the help of God.

As broken as my heart was when I started this journey, I was determined not to stay broken. I was determined that God would get the glory out of what had broken me.

I started attending Divorce Care, a program that promotes healing and recovery after divorce.

I began to pour out to others as I was healing.

Some months after completing the course for the second time, I was asked to join the leadership team.

And I found so much fulfillment in helping others to heal from what I was healing from.

As I was leaving a divorce care event one afternoon, I found myself crying tears of joy.

The fulfillment God had brought to my life as a result of pouring out to others, and the people he had connected me to, were a breath of fresh air.

I had never felt so fulfilled.

And it wasn't because of things.

And it wasn't because of another human person.

It was because I chose to hold on to the raft when everything fell apart, and rebuild.

Brick by brick.

And moment by moment.

And it wasn't easy.

After all that I had been through and all that had been unfair, I thought that surely the process of rebuilding wouldn't take more than a year.

I deserved everything new.

But it didn't happen in a year.

It happened moment after moment.

And over several years.

And I am still rebuilding.

But now, I can see it coming together.

I am no longer holding onto a raft and I have come out of the freezing water.

I see walls and a I see a deck.

And I see the coming together of something beautiful.

And so will you.

As long as you grab onto your raft and hold to it with everything you have.

And moment by moment, use what you have to rebuild.

You've got something left.

And you can rebuild.

CHAPTER 20

Getting over the Middle

There is a game we played as kids called Monkey in the Middle.

I am not a sports person in the least, so it wasn't until I started writing this chapter that I realized that professional athletes still use this game from time to time to warm-up and/or train their players.

When speaking to a professional coach, I learned that the reason Monkey in the Middle is used as a warm-up drill is to give players a chance to practice both their defense and offense techniques.

If you already know the game, I'm sure you can see how that is.

But if you've never heard of or played this game, I will explain it for you now.

There are three players and a ball.

Two players stand on the outside and one stands in the middle.

The two outside players throw the ball to each other while trying to keep it from the middle player – the monkey in the middle.

Meanwhile, it is the job of the player in the middle to do everything they can to grab the ball from one of the outside players to get from the middle to the outside.

And if successful, the player that the monkey in the middle has stolen the ball from is now the monkey that is in the middle.

With two really good outside players, the middle monkey would never make it to the outside.

It's a game of mental skill and physical agility.

Keeping the ball out of the hands of the monkey in the middle.

You may already see where I'm going here, but if you don't, I'm going to land this plane right now.

What you're going through, if you are not careful, it has the capability to steal from you.

And yes, I know we've spent a lot of this book talking about how there's already been so much stolen.

If you're honest, that's probably why you picked up this book in the first place.

You needed something to help you make sense of what had already been lost and stolen.

And now, you get to this chapter, and here I am telling you that you have the capacity to have more taken from you.

But listen, if we don't have this conversation, then I wouldn't really be your friend.

Because this is the conversation that all friends need to have with each other when one knows another has so much at stake and is about to give it all up.

Yes, the middle has had its losses. But the evidence that it hasn't taken the best from you, is you.

You are the proof.

You are proof that your middle is building you and helping you to build.

But if you don't play on the offense of your own life, and if you don't become skilled at moving and making moves even when there is a nagging monkey in the middle aggressively in your face, you could lose out on so much more.

Dictionary.com defines agility as the power of moving quickly and easily; it also defines agility as intellectual acuity.

If we are honest, in some way or another, we are able people with plans.

Some of us have vision boards and written timelines.

Others of us have desires and things we know that we'd like to see happen in our lives.

And when things are going according to plan, we know what next step we need to take.

But when the plan shifts and things get messy, we tend to get off track.

For many of us, we don't move quickly because we become overtaken by the fact that the plan has been ripped to shreds.

For others of us, we move too quick, in line with the previous plans, that we do not even take into account that those plans had been ripped to shreds.

And in both cases, we have failed to move and adjust.

And so, it is easy for the monkey in the middle to steal from us, because we either have stopped throwing the ball altogether, or have not noticed that our other outside player has shifted position and we have stayed stuck throwing the ball in the same direction.

Listen, the mess that life throws us, does in fact shift our plans from time to time.

But a shift in the plan is not a derailment of your ability to create another plan.

The mess in the middle of your life does have an assignment.

Its assignment is to keep you stuck.

But you also have an assignment in the mess of your middle.

And that is to keep moving and to not get stuck.

To be agile and an acute thinker.

To remember that there is always possibility with God.

To stay on the offense.

To be quick on your feet and in your head.

To keep the mess in the middle from securing its assignment.

And to instead give the mess in the middle a new assignment altogether.

To turn the mess that was assigned to steal from you into the drill that strengthened you.

Yes, you can get caught up by the middle.

Yes, the middle can distract you.

Yes, the middle can steal from you.

But you don't have to let it.

Now on your feet, friend. Pay attention to what's happening in the game.

Be nimble.

Switch directions quickly when you have to.

But by all means, stay in the game.

Move your feet.

Play the game.

And keep the ball out of the middle.

CHAPTER 21

A Mess In The Mess

By the time you reach this Chapter, you would've taken quite the journey with me already.

So, you know some of my stuff.

But since we've become good friends by now, I'm going to let you in a little more personally and share with you one of my biggest issues.

Whew… I'm taking a deep breath and here it comes.

When something is out of my control physically, I tend to spiral out of control mentally and emotionally.

I know, I know.

All of these pages of me walking you through your middle, a place where you are essentially out of control, and here I am now admitting to you towards the end of your journey that I do not have it together.

At all.

But see, that's the point.

None of us has it all together.

Not the parent who gave birth to you.

Not the Pastor who preaches from the pulpit to you.

Not the counselor who listens to you.

Not the friend who advises you.

Not the teacher who educates you.

Not the writer who seeks to encourage and enlighten you.

Feel free to lengthen this list as you need.

Because none of us, not a one of us, has it all together.

We are all broken humans trying to find our way home.

And I want you to remember that when you find yourself with this book in your hand, trying to believe the promises of God in your messy middle, but having a moment where you feel defeated.

I want you to remember that when you are encouraging others in their season of defeat, and they seem despondent and withdrawn.

This journey, this thing called life, this thing that knocks us off of our feet and leaves us gasping for air in hopes that we'll be able to breathe deeply again, it is not easy.

It is painful.

It is confusing.

It is blistering.

It is tiring.

But through it all, God is with us.

And He loves us.

And that's the magnificently beautiful part of our messy.

You see, when I act a mess in the middle of my mess, God does not abandon me.

He lets me take my moments.

As long as I need them to be.

And when I am ready to reach for His hand and ask Him to guide me through my mess, He reaches for me at the very moment I call.

Because He's a good God.

A loving God.

A faithful God.

A patient God.

And He will not abandon us in our mess, even while we are a mess.

CHAPTER 22

A Testimony in the Mess

When I was grieving the passing of my three-year old daughter, there were a few things I used to dread hearing people say to me. One of those things was that God was going to use what I was going through to help someone else.

In the moments when I had the emotional energy to respond back to that comment, I would quickly say, "I don't want to help anybody else. I just want to not be in this pain."

And at the time, I meant it.

The pain was unbearable.

At first, I couldn't eat at all.

Later on down the line, I ate far too may cupcakes trying to comfort the never-ending ache.

My brain was foggy most days, but I still had go to work and hear other people complain about more trivial things in life.

I was angry.

I was hurting.

And it wasn't that I didn't care about other people.

But I didn't want their help to come at my expense.

And if you would have left it up to me then, I would have been unwilling to even consider the possibility that going through such a loss would somehow still be used for good.

But years later, I see it now.

Clearly, in fact.

Because as a trainer and coach at my place of employment, I have come across so many people struggling through loss of many kinds, and still having to hold it all together.

My ability to break through to them often comes through my place of acknowledgement and understanding.

Others may not know what is like to be walking through life feeling like a piece of you is missing, and still trying to function like you are whole, not at that level, but because I have, I am often able to reach others who are.

And it is encouraging to be able to share with others a version of me that is on that other side of the dark black hole that seemed to swallow me up for years.

Still in the midst of a messy middle, yes, but out of the black hole.

And the hope of my smile and my existence is hope for them.

Out of a messy middle, came a testimony.

A testimony of hope.

And it's a hope I share with others.

It's a hope I share with you.

But it's also a hope that you will have to share as you wade through the mess of your middle.

I know you may not see it now.

I know you don't even want to be here now.

I know you may not even want to think of helping another single soul now.

But just keep wading through the mess in your middle.

Pretty soon, your life and the story of it all will be someone else's hope, when they too, have to wade through a messy middle.

CHAPTER 23

A Stinky Dead Mess

When I started writing this book, I started it out taking into consideration some feedback I received from my audience.

Not everyone that reads what I write shares my faith.

And while I never want to water down the truth of the Bible and the message of God's Word, I wanted to write this book in a way that someone who was looking for encouragement and inspiration would be able to read through the pages, still experience God and my relationship with Him, while not becoming overly bogged down by scriptures that may be too much in a single moment.

And so, I intentionally gave you an entire book about my Christian experience walking through the messy middle without scripture.

That is, up until this point.

Because as a Christian, I have not fulfilled my purpose if I give you a book full of my experience as if I am the authority on life (which I am not) and have not led you to the authority of my life.

And so, I wanted to talk about a story in the Bible that was messy.

And I mean stinky, messy.

It's a story found in John 11 about a woman named Martha.

Now, I know most Bible scholars reading this are going to immediately call me out.

They are likely going to try to tell me that this story isn't about Martha at all, it's about Lazarus.

I'm going to beg to differ, however, because Lazurus was dead, and it was Martha who was in the middle.

And yes, I know I'm getting ahead of myself here, so let me just slow down and tell you the story.

A man in the Bible named Lazarus was very ill, and because his sisters had both been in the presence of Jesus before, they didn't hesitate to find Him.

They knew that Jesus also loved Lazarus and so it would only make sense that when they told Jesus that Lazarus was ill, Jesus would come running. But instead, Jesus did nothing.

Well... I wouldn't exactly say nothing.

What He did was give Martha a Word.

He told Martha the sickness that Lazarus had, would not lead to death, but that it would all be for God's glory.

And then, Jesus went back to what He was doing. Not just for a moment, but for two whole days.

After two days, Jesus and His disciples traveled back to where Lazarus was.

But understand, we're talking about Bible days now.

This travel wasn't by car, bus, or train, so by the time that Jesus got to Lazarus, Lazarus was already dead, and he had been dead for four days.

When Martha, one of the sisters of Lazarus, saw Jesus, she went to meet Him, and she said these words, "Lord, if you had been here, my brother would not have died."

Now this is a messy middle if I've ever seen one.

The brother that you wanted to live has died. And the one person that you knew could heal Him waited to come to see Him until it seemed like it was too late.

That same person spoke and told you that the sickness your brother had would not kill him, but yet, there your brother was, in the tomb dead.

And Martha, has two choices.

She could either believe that it is over, because it looks over.

Or she could believe that a miracle was possible, even in the midst of it looking as if it was over.

After all, Jesus was present in her midst.

Jesus, yes Jesus was there in the middle of the mess.

Jesus was there after the sickness that He said wouldn't cause Lazarus to die, had in fact caused Lazarus die.

And there Lazarus was with a body that looked dead, laying in a tomb, and by now, stinking and smelling like death, for four days.

Oh, it was a mess.

But it was a mess Jesus seemed to be happy about, oddly enough.

Because just a few verses up before Martha meets Jesus, Jesus speaks to His disciples and tells them that He is in fact glad that He wasn't present when Lazarus died, for their sakes, He said, so that they could believe.

Hmmm... believe.

Now, the disciples had walked with Jesus long enough to see Him do miracles.

I don't think that any of them doubted His power to heal.

But what I think is that in this moment, when the situation was beyond just needing a healing, and when it was messy, and stinky, and rotten to the core, Jesus wanted them to believe that even then, a resurrection, a calling up out of stinky, rotten death was still possible.

And perhaps this is why, even when Jesus knew that Lazarus was dead, He said that Lazarus was only sleeping.

I'm not sure which option you would've chosen had you been Martha.

I'm going to be honest and say that I probably would've thought it was too late for anything to be done in that situation.

I probably would have been ready to accept the death of it all in that moment.

After all, it had been days since Lazarus had been dead, and He was starting to stink.

But Martha knew the power of Jesus, even in the middle of a rotten, stinky, messy, middle.

And she said to Jesus, "Even now, I know that whatever you ask God, God will give you." (Verse 22)

Jesus tells her that Lazarus will again live.

By now, even if you don't know the Bible story, you have probably already figured out that Lazarus does indeed live.

But there are still some events before Jesus calls Lazarus out of the tomb.

There's Mary, the other sister of Lazarus who also tells Jesus that if He had come sooner, Lazarus would not have died.

There is grief.

Mary cries. Martha cries. Their friends cry.

And Jesus cries.

After all, Jesus loved Lazarus, too.

But I have to say that I have always found that interesting.

That Jesus knew that Lazarus would live again, but still He cried at Lazarus' death.

There's just so much to unpack there.

The fact that even Jesus who is an all-spiritual being wrapped up in flesh had a human moment when He witnessed death, when He witnessed loss, when He was faced with a stinky, rotten, messy, middle.

And so yes, this is the part where I go back to telling you that it is okay to have your human moments and your human emotions and grieve, and cry, and be disappointed, because you are human.

But don't forget to do what Martha did and recognize the presence of Jesus.

Because when Jesus is present, resurrection is possible.

Yes, even in the middle of a messy, stinky, rotten, mess.

And I guess that's where we end this all.

Right here, at the feet of Jesus.

Because He's present.

In our hopelessness.

In our despair.

In our faults.

In our weaknesses.

In our downfalls.

In our mess.

And as long as He is present, so much is possible.

A PRAYER FOR YOU IN THE MESSY MIDDLE

Dear Lord,

My friend is in the middle of a place that seems messy and without hope. Some days, it is all they can do to find the strength to climb out of bed and face another day. They don't see a way out of their messy situation. But I know that you do. So Father, what I ask of you today is to be the sweet smelling aroma calling my friend forward out of their dark, stinky place. Be the gentle voice in their ear that coaches them through their hard, reminding them that if they just keep pushing, they will make it through their middle. Be the forgiveness that they need when they sit in anguish over the parts of the mess that they created. Be the peace they need when chaos is around them and they need a place of solace within them. Hold their hand when they feel lonely. And hold their hearts when they are hurting. Remind them of your promises over and over again. And remind them of your presence. Because when you are present, miracles are possible. When you are present, our messy middle, turns into sweet tasting goodness. So Father, be ever present with my friend, in their messy middle. In Jesus' Name, Amen.

ACKNOWLEDGEMENT

Many people have taken this journey with me, but my very best friend has walked with me through most of every high and every low. So to the person in my Target story, my best friend Kenisha, thank you for your friendship. Your consistency in being present even when you had no words has been life giving to me. And I thank God for you and your family every day.

To the friends in my holiday story, the Warrens, your home has been a home where I sat on the floor and cried like a baby many days. It's been My get away for friendship coffee breaks with Susan, but also my family still, even when my family was breaking apart. I love you so much!

To my Divorce Care family, and every friend that poured into me and helped me to realize that I had more to pour when I wanted to walk into a cave and stay, until it became my grave, thank you.

God sent me life-lines and each and every one of you were it.

I love you so very much.

And my prayer is not only that this book is an encouragement to you and others in your lives, but that it is evidence that your encouragement and your presence and your love and your time was not spent in vain.

Printed in the United States
by Baker & Taylor Publisher Services